GW01081156

POETRY
— TO —
SHARE
YOUR
LOVE

For Nathaniel and Ashley Schmidt
For Matthew and Michelle Schmidt
and for Natalia
with love

POETRY
— TO —
SHARE YOUR LOVE

Compiled by Michael Schmidt

MQP

Contents

Preface

This anthology, drawn mainly from the poetry of the seventeenth century to the present day, traces every stage of human love, from first passion to last rites, and in every variety and age of love. It is organized around one of the oldest and most cherished images of passion. Love flares up, burns, and dies down. The spark is the beginning and ashes are the end. No phase, even when the fire is false, is without its crackling, sparkling, flashing—and its humor.

Love takes men and women as high and as low as they can go, without recourse to God. The love of God is omitted from this book because in poetry, except for the great mystics with their peculiar and inimitable exercises, the divine and the carnal are not easy bedfellows. Even a charming little god like Cupid will not let Psyche look upon his feathery limbs. He appears in this book only on sufferance, because Ezra Pound tucked the two up together in one of the loveliest lyrics in the language.

Omar Khayyam, with the assistance of that great nineteenth century poet-translator Edward Fitzgerald, wrote in 'The Rubaiyyat' four of the most famous love-lines in English:

Here with a Loaf of Bread beneath the Bough,
A Flask of Wine, a Book of Verse – and Thou
Beside me singing in the Wilderness –
And Wilderness is Paradise enow.

You provide the loaf, the bough and the flask of wine. Let this be the book of verse. It will delight, instruct, inflame, empower and, where necessary, console.

If the flames of love rise up and then die down, even in the final stages there are passions and sensations. The ash never quite cools, and what happens at the end of an encounter, an affair or a long partnership can be as mysterious and charged as the first dazzlement.

Michael Schmidt

The coming of light

Even this late it happens:
the coming of love, the coming of light.
You wake and the candles are lit as if by themselves,
stars gather, dreams pour into your pillows,
sending up warm bouquets of air.
Even this late the bones of the body shine
and tomorrow's dust flares into breath.

Mark Strand

To Eros

In that I loved you, Love, I worshipped you,
In that I worshipped well, I sacrificed
All of most worth. I bound and burnt and slew
Old peaceful lives; frail flowers; firm friends; and Christ.

I slew all falser loves; I slew all true,
That I might nothing love but your truth, Boy.
Fair fame I cast away as bridegrooms do
Their wedding garments in their haste of joy.

But when I fell upon your sandalled feet,
You laughed; you loosed away my lips; you rose.
I heard the singing of your wing's retreat;
Far-flown, I watched you flush the Olympian snows
Beyond my hoping. Starkly I returned
To stare upon the ash of all I burned.

Wilfred Owen

'Many red devils ran from my heart'

Many red devils ran from my heart
And out upon the page.
They were so tiny
The pen could mash them.
And many struggled in the ink.
It was strange
To write in this red muck
Of things from my heart.

Stephen Crane

The first day

I wish I could remember the first day,
First hour, first moment of your meeting me,
If bright or dim the season, it might be
Summer or winter for aught I can say
So unrecorded did it slip away,
So blind was I to see and to foresee,
So dull to mark the budding of my tree
That would not blossom for many a May.
If only I could recollect it! Such
A day of days! I let it come and go
As traceless as a thaw of bygone snow.
It seemed to mean so little, meant so much!
If only now I could recall that touch,
First touch of hand in hand! – Did one but know!

Christina Rossetti

Recuerdo

We were very tired, we were very merry –
We had gone back and forth all night upon the ferry.
It was bare and bright, and smelled like a stable –
But we looked into a fire, we leaned across a table,
We lay on the hill-top underneath the moon;
And the whistles kept blowing, and the dawn came soon.

We were very tired, we were very merry –
We had gone back and forth all night on the ferry;
And you ate an apple, and I ate a pear,
From a dozen of each we had bought somewhere;
And the sky went wan, and the wind came cold,
And the sun rose dripping, a bucketful of gold.

We were very tired, we were very merry,
We had gone back and forth all night on the ferry.
We hailed, "Good morrow, mother!" to a shawl-covered
    head,
And bought a morning paper, which neither of us read;
And she wept, "God bless you!" for the apples and the
    pears,
And we gave her all our money but our subway fares.

Edna St. Vincent Millay

Speech for Psyche
in the golden book of Apuleius

All night, and as the wind lieth among
The cypress trees, he lay,
Nor held me save as air that brusheth by one
Close, and as the petals of flowers in falling
Waver and seem not drawn to earth, so he
Seemed over me to hover light as leaves
And closer me than air,
And music flowing through me seemed to open
Mine eyes upon new colors.
O winds, what wind can match the weight of him!

Ezra Pound

Sunday morning apples

To William Sommer

The leaves will fall again sometime and fill
The fleece of nature with those purposes
That are your rich and faithful strength of line.

But now there are challenges to spring
In that ripe nude with head reared
Into a realm of swords, her purple shadow
Bursting on the winter of the world
From whiteness that cries defiance to the snow.

A boy runs with a dog before the sun, straddling
Spontaneities that form their independent orbits,
Their own perennials of light
In the valley where you live
                              (called Brandywine).

I have seen the apples there that toss you secrets,–
Beloved apples of seasonable madness
That feed your inquiries with aerial wine.

Put them them beside a pitcher with a knife,
And poise them full and ready for explosion –
The apples, Bill, the apples!

Hart Crane

Some trees

These are amazing: each
Joining a neighbor, as though speech
Were a still performance.
Arranging by chance

To meet as far this morning
From the world as agreeing
With it, you and I
Are suddenly what the trees try

To tell us we are:
That their merely being there
Means something; that soon
We may touch, love, explain.

And glad not to have invented
Such comeliness, we are surrounded:
A silence already filled with noises,
A canvas on which emerges

A chorus of smiles, a winter morning.
Placed in a puzzling light, and moving,
Our days put on such reticence
These accents seem their own defense.

John Ashbery

Stolen moments

What happened, happened once. So now it's best
in memory – an orange he sliced: the skin
unbroken, then the knife, the chilled wedge
lifted to my mouth, his mouth, the thin
membrane between us, the exquisite orange,
tongue, orange, my nakedness and his,
the way he pushed me up against the fridge –
Now I get to feel his hands again, the kiss
that didn't last, but sent some neural twin
flashing wildly through the cortex. Love's
merciless, the way it travels in
and keeps emitting light. Beside the stove
we ate an orange. And there were purple flowers
on the table. And we still had hours.

Kim Addonizio

Poem 1 from twenty poems of love

Body of a woman, white hills, white thighs,
you look like a world, lying in surrender.
My rough peasant's body digs in you
and makes the son leap from the depth of the earth.

I only was a tunnel. The birds fled from me,
and night swamped me with its crushing invasion.
To survive myself I forged you like a weapon,
like an arrow in my bow, a stone in my sling.

But the hour of vengeance falls, and I love you.
Body of skin, of moss, of eager and firm milk.
Oh the goblets of the breasts! Oh the eyes of absence!
Oh the roses of the pubis! Oh your voice, slow and sad!

Body of a woman, I will persist in your grace.
My thirst, my boundless desire, my shifting road.
Dark river-beds where the eternal thirst flows
and weariness follows, and the infinite ache.

Pablo Neruda
(Translated from the Spanish by W. S. Merwin)

Soft, to your places

Soft, to your places, animals,
Your legendary duty calls.
     It is, to be
Lucky for my love and me.
     And yet we have seen that all's
A fiction that is heard of love's difficulty.

And what if the simple primrose show
That mighty work went on below
     Before it grew
A moral miracle for us two?
     Since of ourselves we know
Beauty to be an easy thing, this will do.

But O when beauty's brought to pass
Will time set down his hour-glass
     And rest content,
His hand upon that monument?
     Unless it is so, alas
That the heart's calling is but to go stripped and diffident.

Soft, to your places, love; I kiss
because it is, because it is.

Thomas Kinsella

Love without hope

Love without hope, as when the young bird-catcher
Swept off his tall hat to the Squire's own daughter,
So let the imprisoned larks escape and fly
Singing about her head, as she rode by.

Robert Graves

Romance

I.

We aren't serious when we're seventeen.
— One fine evening, to hell with beer and lemonade,
Noisy cafes with their shining lamps!
We walk under the green linden trees of the park.

The lindens smell good in the good June evenings!
At times the air is so scented that we close our eyes.
The wind laden with sounds – the town isn't far –
Has the smell of grapevines and beer...

II.

There you can see a very small patch
Of dark blue, framed by a little branch,
Pinned up by a naughty star, that melts
In gentle quivers, small and very white...

Night in June! Seventeen! – We are overcome by it all.
The sap is champagne and goes to our head...
We talked a lot and feel a kiss on our lips
Trembling there like a small insect

III.

Our wild heart moves through novels like Crusoe,
When, in the light of a pale street lamp,
A girl goes by attractive and charming
Under the shadow of her father's terrible collar...

And as she finds you incredibly naïve,
While clicking her little boots,
She turns abruptly and in a lively way…
– Then cavatinas die on your lips…

        IV.
You are in love. Occupied until the month of August.
You are in love. – Your sonnets make Her laugh.
All your friends go off, you are ridiculous.
— Then one evening the girl you worshipped deigned to
    write to you!

That evening…you return to the bright cafés,
You ask for beer or lemonade…
We're not serious when we are seventeen
And when we have green linden trees in the park.

Arthur Rimbaud
(Translated from the French by Wallace Fowlie)

Alone for a week

I washed a load of clothes
and hung them out to dry.
Then I went up to town
and busied myself all day.
The sleeve of your best shirt
rose ceremonious
when I drove in; our night-
clothes twined and untwined in
a little gust of wind.
For me it was getting late;
for you, where you were, not.
The harvest moon was full
but sparse clouds made its light
not quite reliable.
The bed on your side seemed
as wide and flat as Kansas;
your pillow plump, cool,
and allegorical…

Jane Kenyon

Love song

Sweep the house clean,
hang fresh curtains
in the windows
put on a new dress
and come with me!
The elm is scattering
its little loaves
of sweet smells
from a white sky!
Who shall hear of us
in the time to come?
Let him say there was
a burst of fragrance
from black branches.

William Carlos Williams

Upon Julia's clothes

When as in silks my Julia goes,
Then, then (methinks) how sweetly flows
That liquefaction of her clothes.
Next, when I cast mine eyes and see
That brave vibration each way free,
O how that glittering taketh me!

Robert Herrick

To Celia

I.
Drink to me only with thine eyes
And I will pledge with mine.
Or leave a kiss within the cup
And I'll not look for wine.
The thirst that from the soul doth rise
Doth ask a drink divine;
But might I of Jove's nectar sup,
I would not change for thine.

II.
I sent thee late a rosy wreath,
Not so much hon'ring thee
As giving it a hope that there
It could not withered be;
But thou thereon did'st only breathe,
And sent'st it back to me,
Since when it grows and smells, I swear
Not of itself, but thee.

Ben Jonson

'Going to Him! Happy letter!'

Going to Him! Happy letter!
Tell Him
Tell Him the page I didn't write
Tell Him – I only said the Syntax
And left the Verb and the pronoun out –
Tell Him just how the fingers hurried
Then – how they waded – slow – slow
And then you wished you had eyes in your pages
So you could see what moved them so

Tell Him – it wasn't a Practised Writer –
You guessed – from the way the sentence toiled
You could hear the Bodice tug, behind you
As if it held but the might of a child
You almost pitied it – you – it worked so
Tell Him – no – you may quibble there –
For it would split His Heart, to know it
And then you and I, were silenter.

Tell Him – Night finished – before we finished
And the Old Clock kept neighing 'Day'!
And you – got sleepy – and begged to be ended –
What could it hinder so – to say?
Tell Him – just how she sealed you – Cautious!
But – if He ask where you are hid
Until tomorrow – Happy letter!
Gesture Coquette – and shake your Head!

Emily Dickinson

Song ('Go, lovely rose')

Go, lovely rose,
Tell her that wastes her time and me,
That now she knows,
When I resemble her to thee,
How sweet and fair she seems to be.

Tell her that's young,
And shuns to have her graces spied,
That had'st thou sprung
In deserts, where no men abide,
Thou must have uncommended died.

Small is the worth
Of beauty from the !ight retired:
Bid her come forth,
Suffer herself to be desired,
And not blush so to be admired.

Then die, that she
The common fate of all things rare
May read in thee;
How small a part of time they share
That are so wondrous sweet and fair.

Edmund Waller

A red, red rose

My luve is like a red, red rose,
That's newly sprung in June.
My luve is like the melodie,
That's sweetly played in tune.

As fair art thou, my bonnie lass,
So deep in luve am I,
And I will luve thee still, my dear,
Till a' the seas gang dry.
   [repeat]

Till a' the seas gang dry, my dear,
And the rocks melt wi' the sun!
And I will luve thee still, my dear,
While the sands o' life shall run.

And fare thee weel, my only luve,
And fare thee weel a while!
And I will come again, my luve,
Though it were ten thousand mile!
   [repeat]

Robert Burns

'All in green went my love riding'

All in green went my love riding
on a great horse of gold
into the silver dawn.

four lean hounds crouched low and smiling
the merry deer ran before.

Fleeter be they than dappled dreams
the swift sweet deer
the red rare deer.

Four red roebuck at a white water
the cruel bugle sang before.

Horn at hip went my love riding
riding the echo down
into the silver dawn.

four lean hounds crouched low and smiling
the level meadows ran before.

Softer be they than slippered sleep
the lean lithe deer
the fleet flown deer.

Four fleet does at a gold valley
the famished arrow sang before.

Bow at belt went my love riding
riding the mountain down
into the silver dawn.

four lean hounds crouched low and smiling
the sheer peaks ran before.

Paler be they than daunting death
the sleek slim deer
the tall tense deer.

Four tell stags at a green mountain
the lucky hunter sang before.

All in green went my love riding
on a great horse of gold
into the silver dawn.

four lean hounds crouched low and smiling
my heart fell dead before.

e. e. cummings

San Antonio

Tonight I lingered over your name,
the delicate assembly of vowels
a voice inside my head.
You were sleeping when I arrived.
I stood by your bed
and watched the sheets rise gently.
I knew what slant of light
would make you turn over.
It was then I felt
the highways slide out of my hands.
I remembered the old men
in the west side cafe,
dealing dominoes like magical charms.
It was then I knew,
like a woman looking backward,
I could not leave you,
or find anyone I loved more.

Naomi Shihab Nye

Girlfriends

That hot September night, we slept in a single bed,
naked, and on our frail bodies the sweat
cooled and renewed itself. I reached out my arms
and you, hands on my breasts, kissed me. Evening of
      amber.

Our nightgowns lay on the floor where you fell to your
knees and became ferocious, pressed your head to my
      stomach,
your mouth to the red gold, the pink shadows; except
I did not see it like this at the time, but arched

my back and squeezed water from the sultry air
with my fists. Also I remembered hearing, clearly
but distantly, a siren some streets away – de

da de da de da – which mingled with my own
absurd cries, so that I looked up, even then,
to see my fingers counting themselves, dancing.

Carol Ann Duffy

I want

...only your hot heart
and nothing more.

       My paradise a field
without a nightingale
or lyres,
with an unobtrusive stream
and a modest fountainhead.

       Without the spur of breeze
troubling the leaves,
without the star that longs
itself to be a leaf.
       One enormous light

to be
the firefly
of one bigger still,
in a field of broken gazes.

A clear place of repose
and there our kissing,
loud specks shed by
echo,
would flower far abroad.

And your hot heart
and nothing more.

Federico García Lorca
(Translated from the Spanish by Michael Schmidt)

The passionate shepherd to his love

Come live with me and be my love
And we will all the pleasures prove
That Valleys, groves, hills and fields,
Woods, or steepy mountain yields.

And we will sit upon the Rocks
Seeing the Shepherds feed their flocks,
By shallow Rivers, to whose falls
Melodious birds sings Madrigals.

And I will make thee beds of Roses
And a thousand fragrant posies,
A cap of flowers, and a kirtle
Embroidered all with leaves of Myrtle.

A gown made of the finest wool
Which from our pretty Lambs we pull,
Fair lined slippers for the cold:
With buckles of the purest gold.

A belt of straw and Ivy buds
With Coral clasps and Amber studs,
And if these pleasures may thee move,
Come live with me and be my love.

The Shepherds' Swains shall dance and sing
For thy delight each May-morning.
If these delights thy mind may move,
Then live with me and be my love.

Christopher Marlowe

To his coy mistress

Had we but world enough, and time,
This coyness, Lady, were no crime.
We would sit down, and think which way
To walk, and pass our long love's day.
Thou by the Indian Ganges' side
Should'st rubies find; I by the tide
Of Humber would complain. I would
Love you ten years before the Flood:
And you should, if you please, refuse
Till the conversion of the Jews.
My vegetable love should grow
Vaster than empires, and more slow;
An hundred years should go to praise
Thine eyes, and on thy forehead gaze;
Two hundred to adore each breast,
But thirty thousand to the rest.
An age at least to every part,
And the last age should show your heart.
For, Lady, you deserve this state,
Nor would I love at lower rate.

　　But at my back I always hear
Time's wingèd chariot hurrying near;
And yonder all before us lie
Deserts of vast eternity.
Thy beauty shall no more be found,
Nor, in thy marble Vault, shall sound

My echoing song; then worms shall try
That long preserved virginity,
And your quaint honor turn to dust,
And into ashes all my lust.
The grave's a fine and private place,
But none I think do there embrace.
    Now therefore, while the youthful hew
Sits on thy skin like morning dew,
And while thy willing soul transpires
At every pore with instant fires,
Now let us sport us while we may;
And now, like amorous birds of prey,
Rather at once our time devour
Than languish in his slow-chapped power.
Let us roll all our strength, and all
Our sweetness, up into one ball
And tear our pleasures with rough strife
Thorough the iron gates of life.
Thus, though we cannot make our sun
Stand still, yet we will make him run.

Andrew Marvell

Lay your sleeping head, my love

Lay your sleeping head, my love,
Human on my faithless arm;
Time and fevers burn away
Individual beauty from
Thoughtful children, and the grave
Proves the child ephemeral:
But in my arms till break of day
Let the living creature lie,
Mortal, guilty, but to me
The entirely beautiful.

Soul and body have no bounds:
To lovers as they lie upon
Her tolerant enchanted slope
In their ordinary swoon,
Grave the vision Venus sends
Of supernatural sympathy,
Universal love and hope;
While an abstract insight wakes
Among the glaciers and the rocks
The hermit's sensual ecstasy.

Certainty, fidelity
On the stroke of midnight pass
Like vibrations of a bell,
And fashionable madmen raise
Their pedantic boring cry:
Every farthing of the cost,
All the dreadful cards foretell,
Shall be paid, but not from this night
Not a whisper, not a thought,
Not a kiss nor look be lost.

Beauty, midnight, vision dies:
Let the winds of dawn that blow
Softly round your dreaming head
Such a day of sweetness show
Eye and knocking heart may bless.
Find the mortal world enough;
Noons of dryness see you fed
By the involuntary powers,
Nights of insult let you pass
Watched by every human love.

W. H. Auden

Vitae summa brevis spem nos vetat incohare longam

They are not long, the weeping and the laughter,
        Love and desire and hate:
I think they have no portion in us after
        We pass the gate.

They are not long, the days of wine and roses:
        Out of a misty dream
Our path emerges for a while, then closes
        Within a dream.

Ernest Christopher Dowson

Assurance

Last night I slept, and when I woke her kiss
Still floated on my lips. For we had strayed
Together in my dream, through some dim glade,
Where the shy moonbeams scarce dared light our bliss.
The air was dank with dew, between the trees,
The hidden glow-worms kindled and were spent.
Cheek pressed to cheek, the cool, the hot night-breeze
Mingled our hair, our breath, and came and went,
As sporting with our passion. Low and deep
Spake in mine ear her voice: 'And didst thou dream,
This could be buried? This could be sleep?
And love be thrall to death! Nay, whatso seem,
Have faith, dear heart; *this is the thing that is!*'
Thereon I woke, and on my lips her kiss.

Emma Lazarus

La Figlia che Piange

O quam te memorem virgo…

Stand on the highest pavement of the stair –
Lean on a garden urn –
Weave, weave the sunlight in your hair –
Clasp your flowers to you with a pained surprise –
Fling them to the ground and turn
With a fugitive resentment in your eyes:
But weave, weave the sunlight in your hair.

So I would have had him leave,
So I would have had her stand and grieve,
So he would have left
As the soul leaves the body torn and bruised,
As the mind deserts the body it has used.
I should find
Some way incomparably light and deft,
Some way we both should understand,
Simple and faithless as a smile and shake of the hand.

She turned away, but with the autumn weather
Compelled my imagination many days,
Many days and many hours:
Her hair over her arms and her arms full of flowers.
And I wonder how they should have been together!
I should have lost a gesture and a pose.
Sometimes these cogitations still amaze
The troubled midnight and the noon's repose.

T. S. Eliot

Haere Ra

Farewell to Hiruharama –
The green hills and the river fog
Cradling the convent and the Maori houses –

The peach tree at my door is broken, sister,
It carried too much fruit,
It hangs now by a bent strip of bark –

But better that way than the grey moss
Cloaking the branch like an old man's beard;
We are broken by the Love of the Many

And then we are at peace
Like the fog, like the river, like a roofless house
That lets the sun stream in because it cannot help it.

James K. Baxter

Navajo bracelet

I'VE GOT A NAVAJO BRACELET THAT
SHIMMERS WHEN I SING.
I've got a Navajo bracelet that shimmers when I sing.
I've got hands all over you and I feel everything.

You put your sweet body in my face
and what I smell is skinny love and lace.

This airplane flight is coming straight and true.
The ropes have left my fingers black and blue.

The desert dust is in my hair.
My eyes have got the canyon stare.

– And I'm flying to the sunlight of your face.

Michael McClure

Your heartbreak

No one else is having your heartbreak.
Your perfect pulsing peach
in scarlet syrup,
your creamy self
pitying.

Not even when the whole world
is stacked like chairs
and you are milky-eyed
with sleep, honey, chocolate,
blues before bedtime.

Right here, where your hand is,
all yours. A beautiful, bleeding,
sprouting red roses,
picked in two halves
from the heartbreak tree,
heartbreak.

It is your prize, you've earned it,
heaved it up
from the wishing well
of your throat,
held its broken body,
treasured it, fed it with tears
the size of cupcakes
and nights like shining spoons.

No one else is having your heartbreak.
Or the way it makes the sound of horses' hooves
if you hold a piece in either hand
and bang it together like a coconut.

Caroline Bird

Juke box love song

I could take the Harlem night
and wrap around you,
Take the neon lights and make a crown,
Take the Lenox Avenue busses,
Taxis, subways,
And for your love song tone their rumble down.
Take Harlem's heartbeat,
Make a drumbeat,
Put it on a record, let it whirl,
And while we listen to it play,
Dance with you till day –
Dance with you, my sweet brown Harlem girl.

Langston Hughes

Final soliloquy of the interior paramour

Light the first light of evening, as in a room
In which we rest and, for small reason, think
The world imagined is the ultimate good.

This is, therefore, the intensest rendezvous.
It is in that thought that we collect ourselves,
Out of all the indifferences, into one thing:

Within a single thing, a single shawl
Wrapped tightly round us, since we are poor, a warmth,
A light, a power, the miraculous influence.

Here, now, we forget each other and ourselves.
We feel the obscurity of an order, a whole,
A knowledge, that which arranged the rendezvous.

Within its vital boundary, in the mind.
We say God and the imagination are one…
How high that highest candle lights the dark.

Out of this same light, out of the central mind,
We make a dwelling in the evening air,
In which being there together is enough.

Wallace Stevens

Happiness

A man and a woman lie on a white bed.
It is morning. I think
Soon they will waken.
On the bedside table is a vase
of lilies; sunlight
pools in their throats.
I watch him turn to her
as though to speak her name
but silently, deep in her mouth—
At the window ledge,
once, twice,
a bird calls.
And then she stirs; her body
fills with his breath.

I open my eyes; you are watching me.
Almost over this room
the sun is gliding.
Look at your face, you say,
holding your own close to me
to make a mirror.
How calm you are. And the burning wheel
passes gently over us.

Louise Glück

Gold

Pale gold of the walls, gold
of the centers of daisies, yellow roses
pressing from a clear bowl. All day
we lay on the bed, my hand
stroking the deep
gold of your thighs and your back.
We slept and woke
entering the golden room together,
lay down in it breathing
quickly, then
slowly again,
caressing and dozing, your hand sleepily
touching my hair now.
We made in those days
tiny identical rooms inside our bodies
which the men who uncover our graves
will find in a thousand years,
shining and whole.

Donald Hall

Someone talking to himself

Even when first her face,
Younger than any spring,
Older than Pharaoh's grain
And fresh as Phoenix-ashes,
Shadowed under its lashes
Every earthly thing,
There was another place
I saw in a flash of pain:
Off in the fathomless dark
Beyond the verge of love
I saw blind fishes move,
And under a stone shelf
Rode the recusant shark –
Cold, waiting, himself.

Oh, even when we fell,
Clean as a mountain source
And barely able to tell
Such ecstasy from grace,
Into the primal bed
And current of our race,
We knew yet must deny
To what we gathered head:
That music growing harsh,
Trees blotting the sky
Above the roaring course
That in the summer's drought

Slowly would peter out
Into a dry marsh.

Love is the greatest mercy.
A volley of the sun
That lashes all with shade,
That the first day be mended;
And yet, so soon undone,
It is the lover's curse
Till time be comprehended
And the flawed heart unmade.
What can I do but move
From folly to defeat,
And call that sorrow sweet
That teaches us to see
The final face of love
In what we cannot be?

Richard Wilbur

A city seems

A city seems between us. It is only love,
Love like a sorrow still
After a labor, after light.
The crowds are one.
Sleep is a single heart
Filling the old avenues we used to know
With miracles of dark and dread
We dare not go to meet
Save as our own dead stalking
Or as two dreams walking
One tread and terrible,
One cloak of longing in the cold,
Though we stand separate and wakeful
Measuring death in miles between us
Where a city seems and memories
Sleep like a populace.

Laura Riding

'How do I love thee?
Let me count the ways.'

How do I love thee? Let me count the ways.
I love thee to the depth and breadth and height
My soul can reach, when feeling out of sight
For the ends of Being and ideal Grace.
I love thee to the level of every day's
Most quiet need, by sun and candle-light.
I love thee freely, as men strive for Right;
I love thee purely, as they turn from Praise.
I love thee with the passion put to use
In my old griefs, and with my childhood's faith.
I love thee with a love I seemed to lose
With my lost saints, I love thee with the breath,
Smiles, tears, of all my life!– and, if God choose,
I shall but love thee better after death.

Elizabeth Barrett Browning

The good-morrow

I wonder by my troth, what thou, and I
Did, till we loved? Were we not weaned till then?
But sucked on country pleasures, childishly?
Or snorted we in the seven sleepers den?
T'was so; but this, all pleasures fancies be.
If ever any beauty I did see
Which I desired, and got, t'was but a dream of thee.

And now good morrow to our waking souls,
Which watch not one another out of fear;
For love, all love of other sights controls,
And makes one little room an every where.
Let sea-discoverers to new worlds have gone,
Let maps to other, worlds on worlds have shown,
Let us possess one world, each hath one, and is one.

My face in thine eye, thine in mine appears,
And true plain hearts do in the faces rest;
Where can we find two better hemispheres
Without sharp North, without declining West?
Whatever dies, was not mixed equally;
If our two loves be one, or, thou and I
Love so alike, that none do slacken, none can die.

John Donne

A birthday

My heart is like a singing bird
      Whose nest is in a watered shoot;
My heart is like an apple-tree
      Whose boughs are bent with thickset fruit;
My heart is like a rainbow shell
      That paddles in a halcyon sea;
My heart is gladder than all these
      Because my love is come to me.

Raise me a dais of silk and down;
      Hang it with vair and purple dyes;
Carve it in doves and pomegranates,
      And peacocks with a hundred eyes;
Work it in gold and silver grapes,
      In leaves and silver fleurs-de-lys;
Because the birthday of my life
      Is come, my love is come to me.

Christina Rossetti

'Because I liked you better'

Because I liked you better
        Than suits a man to say,
It irked you, and I promised
        To throw the thought away.

To put the world between us
        We parted, stiff and dry;
'Good-bye,' said you, 'forget me.'
        'I will, no fear,' said I.

If here, where clover whitens
        The dead man's knoll, you pass,
And no tall flower to meet you
        Starts in the trefoiled grass,

Halt by the headstone naming
        The heart no longer stirred,
And say the lad that loved you
        Was one that kept his word.

Alfred Edward Housman

Love's secret

Never seek to tell thy love,
Love that never told can be;
For the gentle wind does move
Silently, invisibly.

I told my love, I told my love,
I told her all my heart;
Trembling, cold, in ghastly fears,
Ah! she did depart!

Soon as she was gone from me,
A traveler came by,
Silently, invisibly
He took her with a sigh.

William Blake

Separation

Your absence has gone through me
Like thread through a needle.
Everything I do is stitched with its color.

W. S. Merwin

The couriers

The word of a snail on the plate of a leaf?
It is not mine. Do not accept it.

Acetic acid in a sealed tin?
Do not accept it. It is not genuine.

A ring of gold with the sun in it?
Lies. Lies and a grief.

Frost on a leaf, the immaculate
Cauldron, talking and crackling

All to itself on the top of each
Of nine black Alps.

A disturbance in mirrors,
The sea shattering its gray one –

Love, love, my season.

Sylvia Plath

Villanelle

Every day our bodies separate,
exploded torn and dazed.
Not understanding what we celebrate

we grope through languages and hesitate
and touch each other, speechless and amazed;
and every day our bodies separate

us further from our planned, deliberate
ironic lives. I am afraid, disphased,
not understanding what we celebrate

when our fused limbs and lips communicate
the unlettered power we have raised.
Every day our bodies' separate

routines are harder to perpetuate.
In wordless darkness we learn wordless praise,
Not understanding what we celebrate;

wake to ourselves, exhausted, in the late
morning as the wind tears off the haze,
not understanding how we celebrate
our bodies. Every day we separate.

Marilyn Hacker

Quietly

Lying here quietly beside you,
My cheek against your firm, quiet thighs,
The calm music of Boccherini
Washing over us in the quiet,
As the sun leaves the housetops and goes
Out over the Pacific, quiet –
So quiet the sun moves beyond us,
So quiet as the sun always goes,
So quiet, our bodies, worn with the
Times and the penances of love, our
Brains curled, quiet in their shells, dormant,
Our hearts slow, quiet, reliable
In their interlocked rhythms, the pulse
In your thigh caressing my cheek. Quiet.

Kenneth Rexroth

Sailing

After having loved we lie close together
and at the same time with distance between us
like two sailing ships that enjoy so intensely
their own lines in the dark water they divide
that their hulls
are almost splitting from sheer delight
while racing, out in the blue
under sails which the night wind fills
with flower-scented air and moonlight
– without one of them ever trying
to outsail the other
and without the distance between them
lessening or growing at all.

But there are other nights, where we drift
like two brightly illuminated luxury liners
lying side by side
with the engines shut off, under a strange constellation
and without a single passenger on board:
On each deck a violin orchestra is playing
in honor of the luminous waves.
And the sea is full of old tired ships
which we have sunk in our attempt to reach each other.

Henrik Nordbrandt
*(Translated from the Danish by the author and
Alexander Taylor)*

The ache of marriage

The ache of marriage:

thigh and tongue, beloved,
are heavy with it,
it throbs in the teeth

We look for communion
and are turned away, beloved,
each and each

It is leviathan and we
in its belly
looking for joy, some joy
not to be known outside it

two by two in the ark of
the ache of it.

Denise Levertov

The embrace

You weren't well or really ill yet either;
just a little tired, your handsomeness
tinged by grief or anticipation, which brought
to your face a thoughtful, deepening grace.

I didn't for a moment doubt you were dead.
I knew that to be true still, even in the dream.
You'd been out – at work maybe? –
having a good day, almost energetic.

We seemed to be moving from some old house
where we'd lived, boxes everywhere, things
in disarray: that was the story of my dream,
but even asleep I was shocked out of narrative

by your face, the physical fact of your face:
inches from mine, smooth-shaven, loving, alert.
Why so difficult, remembering the actual look
of you? Without a photograph, without strain?

So when I saw your unguarded, reliable face,
your unmistakable gaze opening all the warmth
and clarity of you – warm brown tea – we held
each other for the time the dream allowed.

Bless you. You came back so I could see you
once more, plainly, so I could rest against you
without thinking this happiness lessened anything,
without thinking you were alive again.

Mark Doty

Non sum qualis eram bonae
sub regno Cynarae

Last night, ah, yesternight, betwixt her lips and mine
There fell thy shadow, Cynara! thy breath was shed
Upon my soul between the kisses and the wine;
And I was desolate and sick of an old passion,
      Yea, I was desolate and bowed my head:
I have been faithful to thee, Cynara! in my fashion.

All night upon mine heart I felt her warm heart beat,
Night-long within mine arms in love and sleep she lay;
Surely the kisses of her bought red mouth were sweet;
But I was desolate and sick of an old passion,
      When I awoke and found the dawn was grey:
I have been faithful to thee, Cynara! in my fashion.

I have forgot much, Cynara! gone with the wind,
Flung roses, roses riotously with the throng,
Dancing, to put thy pale, lost lilies out of mind;
But I was desolate and sick of an old passion,
      Yea, all the time, because the dance was long:
I have been faithful to thee, Cynara! in my fashion.

I cried for madder music and for stronger wine,
But when the feast is finished and the lamps expire,
Then falls thy shadow, Cynara! the night is thine;
And I am desolate and sick of an old passion,
        Yea hungry for the lips of my desire:
I have been faithful to thee, Cynara! in my fashion.

Ernest Christopher Dowson

Y Volver

Who is to say Love
with her battered face
won't come? Who's to know
she won't rise and run
her comb through clotted
hair and spray the scent
of my mysterious apples
between her breasts?

She rises with the strength
of seeds and the rule of roots
riddling the sidewalk.
She is the hag who cries
for hours in the mewing
of lovers. She's the catch
in their sweaty breath,
the blush of rose wine
on the magnolia in winter.

She is her best in ice
when her swelling abides
and small mirrors litter
the lawns. She is the face
you casually scuff through
in the refuse of a storm.
She can't ever hear you
but she sings. She feeds

the blooming magpie
death until he's bloated
with the feast of her
leaving. She is the dried
blood gracing his wings.
Vengeful and forgiving,
her honor weighs in a few
blown stars, in the halo
that lingers in the west
when the launched nightship

explodes, in the one lie
she espouses in her heat,
the beat between her thighs,
the veldt where she holds
you when you mean to go
free. Love, in her candor,
can't explain the attraction
but muzzles the wild
horse's mane, and rides.

Lorna Dee Cervantes

Love in a bathtub

Years later we'll remember the bathtub,
the position
        of the taps
the water, slippery
as if a bucketful
        of eels had joined us…
we'll be old, our children grown up
but we'll remember the water
               sloshing out
the useless soap,
the mountain of wet towels.
'Remember the bathtub in Belfast?'
we'll prod each other –

Sujata Bhatt

'She walks in beauty'

She walks in beauty, like the night
      Of cloudless climes and starry skies;
And all that's best of dark and bright
      Meet in her aspect and her eyes:
Thus mellowed to that tender light
      Which heaven to gaudy day denies.

One shade the more, one ray the less,
      Had half impaired the nameless grace
Which waves in every raven tress,
      Or softly lightens o'er her face;
Where thoughts serenely sweet express
      How pure, how dear their dwelling-place.

And on that cheek, and o'er that brow,
      So soft, so calm, yet eloquent,
The smiles that win, the tints that glow,
      But tell of days in goodness spent,
A mind at peace with all below,
      A heart whose love is innocent!

George Gordon, Lord Byron

Song

Under the lime-tree, on the daisied ground,
      Two that I know of made their bed;
There you may see, heaped and scattered round,
      Grass and blossoms, broken and shed,
All in a thicket down in the dale;
          Tandaradei
Sweetly sang the nightingale.

Ere I set foot in the meadow, already
      Some one was waiting for somebody;
There was a meeting O gracious Lady!
      There is no pleasure again for me.
Thousands of kisses there he took,
          Tandaradei
See my lips, how red they look!

Leaf and blossom he had pulled and piled
      For a couch, a green one, soft and high;
And many a one hath gazed and smiled,
      Passing the bower and pressed grass by;
And the roses crushed hath seen,
          Tandaradei
Where I laid my head between.

In this love passage, if any one had been there,
      How sad and shamed should I be!
But what were we a doing alone among the green there,
      No soul shall ever know except my love and me,
And the little nightingale.
          Tandaradei
She, I think, will tell no tale.

Thomas Lovell Beddoes
(Translated from the German of Walther von der Vogelweide)

Carnal knowledge II

Grasshoppers click and whirr.
Stones grow in the field.
Autumnal warmth is sealed
in a gold skin of light
on darkness plunging down
to earth's black molten core.

Earth has no more to yield.
Her blond grasses are dry.
      Nestling my cheek against
      the hollow of your thigh
      I lay cockeyed with love
      in the most literal sense.

Your eyes, kingfisher blue.
This was the season, this
the light, the halcyon air.
Our window framed this place.
If there were music here,
insectile, abstract, bare,

it would bless no human ear.
Shadows lie with the stones.
Bury our hearts, perhaps
they'll strike it rich with earth's
black marrow, crack, take root,
bring forth vines, blossom, fruit.

    Roses knocked on the glass.
    Wine like a running stream
    no evil spell could cross
    flowed round the house of touch.
God grant me drunkenness
if this is sober knowledge,

song to melt sea and sky
apart, and lift these hills
from the shadow of what was,
and roll them back, and lie
in naked ignorance
in the hollow of your thigh.

Gwen Harwood

The disciple

When Narcissus died the pool of his pleasure changed from a cup of sweet waters into a cup of salt tears, and the Oreads came weeping through the woodland that they might sing to the pool and give it comfort.

And when they saw that the pool had changed from a cup of sweet waters into a cup of salt tears, they loosened the green tresses of their hair and cried to the pool and said, 'We do not wonder that you should mourn in this manner for Narcissus, so beautiful was he.'

'But was Narcissus beautiful?' said the pool.

'Who should know that better than you?' answered the Oreads. 'Us did he ever pass by, but you he sought for, and would lie on your banks and look down at you, and in the mirror of your waters he would mirror his own beauty.'

And the pool answered, 'But I loved Narcissus because, as he lay on my banks and looked down at me, in the mirror of his eyes I saw ever my own beauty mirrored.'

Oscar Wilde

Waiting for Icarus

He said he would be back and we'd drink wine together
He said that everything would be better than before
He said we were on the edge of a new relation
He said he would never again cringe before his father
He said that he was going to invent full-time
He said he loved me that going into me
He said was going into the world and the sky
He said all the buckles were very firm
He said the wax was the best wax
He said Wait for me here on the beach
He said Just don't cry

I remember the gulls and the waves
I remember the islands going dark on the sea
I remember the girls laughing
I remember they said he only wanted to get away from me
I remember mother saying: Inventors are like poets, a
    trashy lot
I remember she told me those who try out inventions are
    worse
I remember she added: Women who love such are the
    worst of all
I have been waiting all day, or perhaps longer.
I would have liked to try those wings myself.
It would have been better than this.

Muriel Rukeyser

A broken appointment

You did not come,
And marching Time drew on, and wore me numb.
Yet less for loss of your dear presence there
Than that I thus found lacking in your make
That high compassion which can overbear
Reluctance for pure loving kindness' sake
Grieved I, when, as the hope-hour stroked its sum,
You did not come.

You love me not,
And love alone can lend you loyalty;
– I know and knew it. But, unto the store
Of human deeds divine in all but name,
Was it not worth a little hour or more
To add yet this: Once you, a woman, came
To soothe a time-torn man; even though it be
You love me not.

Thomas Hardy

Sex without love

How do they do it, the ones who make love
without love? Beautiful as dancers,
gliding over each other like ice-skaters
over the ice, fingers hooked
inside each other's bodies, faces
red as steak, wine, wet as the
children at birth whose mothers are going to
give them away. How do they come to the
come to the come to the God come to the
still waters, and not love
the one who came there with them, light
rising slowly as steam off their joined
skin? These are the true religious,
the purists, the pros, the ones who will not
accept a false Messiah, love the
priest instead of the God. They do not
mistake the lover for their own pleasure,
they are like great runners: they know they are alone
with the road surface, the cold, the wind,
the fit of their shoes, their over-all cardio-
vascular health – just factors, like the partner
in the bed, and not the truth, which is the
single body alone in the universe
against its own best time.

Sharon Olds

To Marguerite

Yes! in the sea of life enisled,
With echoing straits between us thrown,
Dotting the shoreless watery wild,
We mortal millions live *alone*.
The islands feel the enclasping flow,
And then their endless bounds they know.

But when the moon their hollows lights,
And they are swept by balms of spring,
And in their glens, on starry nights,
The nightingales divinely sing;
And lovely notes, from shore to shore,
Across the sounds and channels pour –

Oh! then a longing like despair
Is to their farthest caverns sent;
For surely once, they feel, we were
Parts of a single continent!
Now round us spreads the watery plain –
Oh might our marges meet again!

Who ordered, that their longing's fire
Should be, as soon as kindled, cooled?
Who renders vain their deep desire?
A God, a God their severance ruled!
And bade betwixt their shores to be
The unplumbed, salt, estranging sea.

Matthew Arnold

Penis envy

I envy men who can yearn
with infinite emptiness
toward the body of a woman,

hoping that the yearning
will make a child,
that the emptiness itself
will fertilize the darkness.

Women have no illusions about this,
being at once
houses, tunnels,
cups & cupbearers,
knowing emptiness as a temporary state
between two fullnesses,
& seeing no romance in it.

If I were a man
doomed to that infinite emptiness,
& having no choice in the matter,
I would, like the rest, no doubt,
find a woman
& christen her moonbelly,
madonna, gold-haired goddess
& make her the tent of my longing,
the silk parachute of my lust,
the blue-eyed icon of my sacred sexual itch,
the mother of my hunger.

But since I am a woman,
I must not only inspire the poem
but also type it,
not only conceive the child
but also bear it,
not only bear the child
but also bathe it,
not only bathe the child
but also feed it,
not only feed the child
but also carry it
everywhere, everywhere…

while men write poems
on the mysteries of motherhood.

I envy men who can yearn
with infinite emptiness

Erica Jong

Pygmalion

Pygmalion was an artful man;
Sculpsit and pinxit were his trade.

He would not have a woman in
The confines of his silky bed;

The ones he knew were troublesome.
Still, he admired the female form

And cut another in that shape
But it was marble, rather hard.

He laid it down upon his bed
And drew a purple coverlet

Across its shapely breasts and legs.
However, it did not respond.

He got it up and gave it clothes
And brought it several sorts of toys.

It did not speak a single word
So in despair he said his prayers.

He did not even dare to say
'This marble' or 'this ivory';

He merely said he'd like a girl
Resembling one he'd made himself.

After his prayers the boy went home
And got back to his kissing game.

To his surprise the girl grew warm;
He slobbered and she slobbered back

This was that famous mutual flame.
The worst of all was yet to come.

Although he often wished her back
In silent marble, good and cold,

The bitch retained her human heat,
The conquest of a stone by art.

May Venus keep me from all hope
And let me turn my love to stone.

C. H. Sisson

Dream song 4

Filling her compact & delicious body
with chicken páprika, she glanced at me
twice.
Fainting with interest, I hungered back
and only the fact of her husband & four other people
kept me from springing on her

or falling at her little feet and crying
'You are the hottest one for years of night
Henry's dazed eyes
have enjoyed, Brilliance.' I advanced upon
(despairing) my spumoni. – Sir Bones: is stuffed,
de world, wif feeding girls.

– Black hair, complexion Latin, jewelled eyes
downcast … The slob beside her   feasts … What wonders
is she sitting on, over there?
The restaurant buzzes. She might as well be on Mars.
Where did it all go wrong? There ought to be a law
against Henry.
– Mr. Bones: there is.

John Berryman

Occupational hazard

He has slept with accountants and brokers,
With a cowgirl (well, someone from Healds).
He has slept with non-smokers and smokers
In commercial and cultural fields.

He has slept with book-keepers, book-binders,
Slept with auditors, florists, PAs
Child psychologists, even child minders,
With directors of firms and of plays.

He has slept with the stupid and clever.
He has slept with the rich and the poor
But he sadly admits that he's never
Slept with a poet before.

Real poets are rare, he confesses,
While it's easy to find a cashier.
So I give him some poets' addresses
And consider a change of career.

Sophie Hannah

Bloody men

Bloody men are like bloody buses –

You wait for about a year
And as soon as one approaches your stop
Two or three others appear.
You look at them flashing their indicators,
Offering you a ride.
You're trying to read the destinations,
You haven't much time to decide.
If you make a mistake, there is no turning back.
Jump off, and you'll stand there and gaze
While the cars and the taxis and lorries go by
And the minutes, the hours, the days.

Wendy Cope

Two cures for love

1. Don't see him. Don't phone or write a letter.
2. The easy way: get to know him better.

Dorothy Parker

Words for departure

1.
Nothing was remembered, nothing forgotten.
When we awoke, wagons were passing on the warm
    summer pavements,
The window-sills were wet from rain in the night,
Birds scattered and settled over chimneypots
As among grotesque trees.
Nothing was accepted, nothing looked beyond.
Slight-voiced bells separated hour from hour,
The afternoon sifted coolness
And people drew together in streets becoming deserted.
There was a moon, and light in a shop-front,
And dusk falling like precipitous water.
Hand clasped hand
Forehead still bowed to forehead –
Nothing was lost, nothing possessed
There was no gift nor denial.

2.
I have remembered you.
You were not the town visited once,
Nor the road falling behind running feet.
You were as awkward as flesh
And lighter than frost or ashes.
You were the rind,
And the white-juiced apple,
The song, and the words waiting for music.

3.
You have learned the beginning;
Go from mine to the other.
Be together; eat, dance, despair,
Sleep, be threatened, endure.
You will know the way of that.
But at the end, be insolent;
Be absurd – strike the thing short off;
Be mad – only do not let talk
Wear the bloom from silence.
And go away without fire or lantern
Let there be some uncertainty about your departure.

Louise Bogan

'They flee from me that sometime did me seek'

They flee from me that sometime did me seek
    With naked foot stalking in my chamber.
I have seen them gentle, tame and meek
    That now are wild and do not remember
    That sometime they put themselves in danger
To take bread at my hand; and now they range
Busily seeking with a continual change.

Thanked be fortune, it hath been otherwise
    Twenty times better; but once in special,
In thin array after a pleasant guise,
    When her loose gown from her shoulders did fall
    And she me caught in her arms long and small,
Therewithal sweetly did me kiss,
And softly said, 'Dear heart, how like you this?'

It was no dream: I lay broad waking.
    But all is turned through my gentleness
Into a strange fashion of forsaking;
    And I have leave to go of her goodness,
    And she also to use newfangleness.
But since that I so kindly am served,
I would fain know what she hath deserved.

Thomas Wyatt

Bilbea

Bilbea, I was in Babylon on Saturday night.
I saw nothing of you anywhere.
I was at the old place and the other girls were there, but no
Bilbea.

Have you gone to another house? or city?
Why don't you write?
I was sorry. I walked home half-sick.

Tell me how it goes.
Send me some kind of a letter.
And take care of yourself.

Carl Sandburg

'Among my friends love is a great sorrow'

Among my friends love is a great sorrow.
It has become a daily burden, a feast,
a gluttony for fools, a heart's famine.
We visit one another asking, telling one another.
We do not burn hotly, we question the fire.
We do not fall forward with our alive
eager faces looking thru into the fire.
We stare back into our own faces.
We have become our own realities.
We seek to exhaust our lovelessness.

Among my friends love is a painful question.
We seek out among the passing faces
a sphinx-face who will ask its riddle.
Among my friends love is an answer to a question
that has not been askt.
Then ask it.

Among my friends love is a payment.
It is an old debt for a borrowing foolishly spent.
And we go on borrowing and borrowing
        from each other.

Among my friends love is a wage
that one might have for an honest living.

Robert Duncan

Never the time and the place

Never the time and the place
   And the loved one all together!
This path how soft to pace!
   This May what magic weather!
Where is the loved one's face?
In a dream that loved one's face meets mine,
   But the house is narrow, the place is bleak
Where, outside, rain and wind combine
   With a furtive ear, if I strive to speak,
   With a hostile eye at my flushing cheek,
With a malice that marks each word, each sign!
O enemy sly and serpentine,
   Uncoil thee from the waking man!
   Do I hold the Past
   Thus firm and fast
Yet doubt if the Future hold I can?
This path so soft to pace shall lead
Through the magic of May to herself indeed!
Or narrow if needs the house must be,
Outside are the storms and strangers: we
Oh, close, safe, warm sleep I and she,
   I and she!

Robert Browning

The prisoner

To-day, Cheng, I touched your face
with two fingers, as a gesture of love;
for I can never prove enough
by sight or sense your strange grace,

but mothwise my hands return
to your fair cheek, as luminous
as a lamp in a paper house,
and touch, to teach love and learn.

I think a hundred hours are gone
that so, like gods, we'd occupy.
But alas, Cheng, I cannot tell why,
to-day I touched a mask stretched on the stone

person of death. There was the urge
to break the bright flesh and emerge
of the ambitious cruel bone.

Keith Douglas

Piazza piece

– I am a gentleman in a dustcoat trying
To make you hear. Your ears are soft and small
And listen to an old man not at all,
They want the young men's whispering and sighing.
But see the roses on your trellis dying
And hear the spectral singing of the moon;
For I must have my lovely lady soon,
I am a gentleman in a dustcoat trying.

– I am a lady young in beauty waiting
Until my truelove comes, and then we kiss.
But what gray man among the vines is this
Whose words are dry and faint as in a dream?
Back from my trellis, Sir, before I scream!
I am a lady young in beauty waiting.

John Crowe Ransom

'Why so pale and wan, fond lover?'

Why so pale and wan, fond lover?
      Prithee why so pale?
Will, when looking well can't move her
      Looking ill prevail?
      Prithee why so pale?

Why so dull and mute, young sinner?
      Prithee why so mute?
Will, when speaking well can't win her,
      Prithee why so mute?

Quit, quit for shame, this will not move,
      This cannot take her;
If of herself she will not love,
      Nothing can make her:
      The devil take her.

Sir John Suckling

'Never more will the wind'

Never more will the wind
cherish you again,
never more will the rain.

Never more
shall we find you bright
in the snow and wind.

The snow is melted,
the snow is gone,
and you are flown:

Like a bird out of our hand,
like a light out of our heart,
you are gone.

H.D. (Hilda Doolittle)

In dream

Black and enduring separation
I share equally with you.
Why weep? Give me your hand,
Promise me you will come again.
You and I are like high
Mountains and we can't move closer.
Just send me word
At midnight sometime through the stars.

Anna Akhmatova
(Translated from the Russian by D. M. Thomas)

'Time does not bring relief;
you all have lied'

Time does not bring relief; you all have lied
      Who told me time would ease me of my pain!
      I miss him in the weeping of the rain;
I want him at the shrinking of the tide;
The old snows melt from every mountain-side,
      And last year's leaves are smoke in every lane;
      But last year's bitter loving must remain
Heaped on my heart, and my old thoughts abide

There are a hundred places where I fear
      To go, – so with his memory they brim
And entering with relief some quiet place
Where never fell his foot or shone his face
I say, "There is no memory of him here!"
      And so stand stricken, so remembering him!

Edna St. Vincent Millay

'I loved you once'

I loved you once. If love is fire, then embers
smoulder in the ashes of this heart.
Don't be afraid. Don't worry. Don't remember.
I do not want you sad now we're apart.

I loved you without language, without hope,
now mad with jealousy, now insecure.
I loved you once so purely, so completely.
I know who loves you next can't love you more.

Alexander Pushkin
(Translated from the Russian by Carol Ann Duffy)

Stop all the clocks

Stop all the clocks, cut off the telephone,
Prevent the dog from barking with a juicy bone,
Silence the pianos and with muffled drum
Bring out the coffin, let the mourners come.

Let aeroplanes circle moaning overhead
Scribbling on the sky the message He Is Dead,
Put crepe bows round the white necks of the public doves,
Let the traffic policemen wear black cotton gloves.

He was my North, my South, my East and West,
My working week and my Sunday rest,
My noon, my midnight, my talk, my song;
I thought that love would last for ever: I was wrong.

The stars are not wanted now: put out every one;
Pack up the moon and dismantle the sun;
Pour away the ocean and sweep up the wood.
For nothing now can ever come to any good.

W. H. Auden

The English lesson

When it was Desdemona's turn to sing
and only minutes of her life remained,
she did not mourn her star, that she had loved:
she sang about a tree, a willow tree.

When it was Desdemona's time to sing,
her voice grew deeper, darker as she sang;
the darkest, coldest demon kept for her
a weeping song of streams through rough beds flowing.

And when it was Ophelia's turn to sing
and only minutes of her life remained,
she was dry as light, as a twig of hay:
wind blew her from the loft into the storm.

And when it was Ophelia's time to sing,
her dreams were waning, all but the dream of death.
Bitter and tired – what tokens sank with her?
In her hair wild celandine, and willows in her arms.

Then letting fall the rags of human passion,
heart-first they plunged into the flowing dark,
fracturing their bodies like white tinder,
silencing their unbroken selves with stars.

Boris Pasternak
(Translated from the Russian by Michael Schmidt)

The voice

Woman much missed, how you call to me, call to me,
Saying that now you are not as you were
When you had changed from the one who was all to me,
But as at first, when our day was fair.

Can it be you that I hear? Let me view you, then,
Standing as when I drew near to the town
Where you would wait for me: yes, as I knew you then,
Even to the original air-blue gown!

Or is it only the breeze, in its listlessness
Travelling across the wet mead to me here,
You being ever dissolved to wan wistlessness,
Heard no more again far or near?

      Thus I; faltering forward,
      Leaves around me falling,
Wind oozing thin through the thorn from norward,
      And the woman calling.

Thomas Hardy

'We learned the Whole of Love'

We learned the Whole of Love –
The Alphabet – the Words
A Chapter – then the mighty Book
Then – Revelation closed

But in Each Other's eyes
An Ignorance beheld
Diviner than the Childhood's
And each to each, a Child

Attempted to expound
What Neither – understood –
Alas, that Wisdom is so large
And Truth – so manifold!

Emily Dickinson

Rose Aylmer

Ah what avails the sceptred race,
      Ah what the form divine!
What every virtue, every grace!
      Rose Aylmer, all were thine.

Rose Aylmer, whom these wakeful eyes
      May weep, but never see,
A night of memories and of sighs
      I consecrate to thee.

Walter Savage Landor

Love song

My own dear love, he is strong and bold
And he cares not what comes after.
His words ring sweet as a chime of gold,
And his eyes are lit with laughter.
He is jubilant as a flag unfurled –
Oh, a gir!, she'd not forget him.
My own dear love, he is all my world, –
And I wish I'd never met him.

My love, he's mad, and my love, he's fleet,
And a wild young wood-thing bore him!
The ways are fair to his roaming feet,
And the skies are sunlit for him.
As sharply sweet to my heart he seems
As the fragrance of acacia.
My own dear love, he is all my dreams, –
And I wish he were in Asia.

My love runs by like a day in June,
And he makes no friends of sorrows.
He'll tread his galloping rigadoon
In the pathway of the morrows.
He'll live his days where the sunbeams start,
Nor could storm or wind uproot him.
My own dear love, he is all my heart, –
And I wish somebody'd shoot him.

Dorothy Parker

The sunlight on the garden

The sunlight on the garden
Hardens and grows cold,
We cannot cage the minute
Within its nets of gold,
When all is told
We cannot beg for pardon.

Our freedom as free lances
Advances towards its end;
The earth compels, upon it
Sonnets and birds descend;
And soon, my friend,
We shall have no time for dances.

The sky was good for flying
Defying the church bells
And every evil iron
Siren and what it tells:
The earth compels,
We are dying, Egypt, dying

And not expecting pardon,
Hardened in heart anew,
But glad to have sat under
Thunder and rain with you,
And grateful too
For sunlight on the garden.

Louis MacNeice

Counting the beats

You, love, and I,
(He whispers) you and I,
And if no more than only you and I
What care you or I ?

Counting the beats,
Counting the slow heart beats,
The bleeding to death of time in slow heart beats,
Wakeful they lie.

Cloudless day,
Night, and a cloudless day,
Yet the huge storm will burst upon their heads one day
From a bitter sky.

Where shall we be,
(She whispers) where shall we be,
When death strikes home, O where then shall we be
Who were you and I ?

Not there but here,
(He whispers) only here,
As we are, here, together, now and here,
Always you and I.

Counting the beats,
Counting the slow heart beats,
The bleeding to death of time in slow heart beats,
Wakeful they lie.

Robert Graves

As we are so wonderfully done with each other

As we are so wonderfully done with each other
We can walk into our separate sleep
On floors of music where the milkwhite cloak of
    childhood lies

Oh my love, my golden lark, my soft long doll
Your lips have splashed my dull house with print of
    flowers
My hands are crooked where they spilled over your dear
    curving

It is good to be weary from that brilliant work
It is being God to feel your breathing under me

A waterglass on the bureau fills with morning…
Don't let anyone in to wake us.

Kenneth Patchen

To my wife

And does the heart grow old? You know
In the indiscriminate green
Of summer or an earliest snow
A landscape is another scene,

Inchoate and anonymous,
And every rock and bush and drift
As our affections alter us
Will alter with the season's shift.

So love by love we come at last,
As through the exclusions of a rhyme,
Or the exactions of a past,
To the simplicity of time,

The antiquity of grace, where yet
We live in terror and delight
With love as quiet as regret
And love like anger in the night.

J. V. Cunningham

The hug

It was your birthday, we had drunk and dined
       Half of the night with our old friend
            Who'd showed us in the end
      To a bed I reached in one drunk stride.
         Already I lay snug,
And drowsy with the wine dozed on one side.

I dozed, I slept. My sleep broke on a hug,
         Suddenly, from behind,
In which the full lengths of our bodies pressed:
         Your instep to my heel,
     My shoulder-blades against your chest.
It was not sex, but I could feel
The whole strength of your body set,
           Or braced, to mine,
        And locking me to you
As if we were still twenty-two
When our grand passion had not yet
        Become familial.
My quick sleep had deleted all
Of intervening time and place.
        I only knew
The stay of your secure firm dry embrace.

Thom Gunn

'When our two souls stand up erect and strong'

When our two souls stand up erect and strong,
Face to face, silent, drawing nigh and nigher,
Until the lengthening wings break into fire
At either curvèd point, what bitter wrong
Can the earth do to us, that we should not long
Be here contented? Think. In mounting higher,
The angels would press on us and aspire
To drop some golden orb of perfect song
Into our deep, dear silence. Let us stay
Rather on earth, Belovèd, where the unfit
Contrarious moods of men recoil away
And isolate pure spirits, and permit
A place to stand and love in for a day,
With darkness and the death-hour rounding it.

Elizabeth Barrett Browning

Love

Dark falls on this mid-western town
where we once lived when myths collided.
Dusk has hidden the bridge in the river
which slides and deepens to become the water
the hero crossed on his way to hell.

Not far from here is our old apartment.
We had a kitchen and an Amish table.
We had a view. And we discovered there
love had the feather and muscle of wings
and had come to live with us,
a brother of fire and air.

We had two infant children one of whom
was touched by death in this town
and spared: and when the hero
was hailed by his comrades in hell
their mouths opened and their voices failed and
there is no knowing what they would have asked
about a life they had shared and lost.

I am your wife.
It was years ago.
Our child was healed. We love each other still.
Across our day-to-day and ordinary distances
we speak plainly. We hear each other clearly.

And yet I want to return to you
on the bridge of the Iowa river as you were,
with snow on the shoulders of your coat
and a car passing with its headlights on:

I see you as a hero in a text –
the image blazing and the edges gilded –
and I long to cry out the epic question
my dear companion:
Will we ever live so intensely again?
Will love come to us again and be
so formidable at rest it offered us ascension
even to look at him?

But the words are shadows and you cannot hear me.
You walk away and I cannot follow.

Eavan Boland

The shampoo

The still explosions on the rocks,
the lichens, grow
by spreading, gray, concentric shocks.
They have arranged
to meet the rings around the moon, although
within our memories they have not changed.

And since the heavens will attend
as long on us,
you've been, dear friend,
precipitate and pragmatical;
and look what happens. For Time is
nothing if not amenable.

The shooting stars in your black hair
in bright formation
are flocking where,
so straight, so soon?
– Come, let me wash it in this big tin basin,
battered and shiny like the moon.

Elizabeth Bishop

A letter to her husband, absent upon publick employment

My head, my heart, mine eyes, my life, nay, more,
My joy, my magazine of earthly store,
If two be one, as surely thou and I,
How stayest thou there, whilst I at Ipswich lie?
So many steps, head from the heart to sever,
If but a neck, soon should we be together,
I, like the Earth this season, mourn in black,
My Sun is gone so far in's zodiac,
Whom whilst I 'joyed, nor storms, nor frost I felt,
His warmth such frigid colds did cause to melt.
My chilled limbs now numbed lie forlorn;
Return, return, sweet Sol, from Capricorn,
In this dead time, alas, what can I more
Than view those fruits which through thy heat I bore?
Which sweet contentment yield me for a space,
True living pictures of their father's face.
O strange effect! now thou art southward gone,
I weary grow the tedious day so long;
But when thou northward to me shalt return,
I wish my Sun may never set, but burn
Within the Cancer of my glowing breast,
The welcome house of him my dearest guest.
Where ever, ever stay, and go not thence,
Till nature's sad decree shall call thee hence;
Flesh of thy flesh, bone of thy bone,
I here, thou there, but both but one.

Anne Bradstreet

The flaw

A seal swims like a poodle through the sheet
of blinding salt. A country graveyard, here
and there a rock, and here and there a pine,
throbs on the essence of the gasoline.
Some mote, some eye-flaw, wobbles in the heat,
hair-thin, hair-dark, the fragment of a hair –

a noose, a question? All is possible;
if there's free will, it's something like this hair,
inside my eye, outside my eye, yet free,
airless as grace, if the good god... I see.
Our bodies quiver. In the rustling air
all's possible, all's unpredictable.

Old wives and husbands! Look, their gravestones wait
in couples with the names and half the date –
one future and one freedom. In a flash,
I see us whiten into skeletons,
our eager, sharpened cries, a pair of stones,
cutting like shark-fins through the boundless wash.

Two walking cobwebs, almost bodiless,
crossed paths here once, kept house, and lay in beds.
Your fingertips once touched my fingertips
and set is tingling through a thousand threads.
Poor pulsing *Fête Champêtre*! The summer slips
between our fingers into nothingness.

We too lean forward, as the heat waves roll
over our bodies, grown insensible,
ready to dwindle off into the soul,
two motes or eye-flaws, the invisible…
Hope of the hopeless launched and cast adrift
on the great flaw that gives the final gift.

Dear Figure curving like a questionmark,
how will you hear my answer in the dark?

Robert Lowell

Time passing, beloved

Time passing, and the memories of love
Coming back to me, carissima, no more mockingly
Than ever before; time passing, unslackening,
Unhastening, steadily; and no more
Bitterly, beloved, the memories of love
Coming into the shore.

How will it end? Time passing and our passages of love
As ever, beloved, blind
As ever before; time binding, unbinding
About us; and yet to remember
Never less chastening, nor the flame of love
Less like an amber.

What will become of us? Time
Passing, beloved, and we in a sealed
Assurance unassailed
By memory. How can it end,
This siege of a shore that no misgivings have steeled,
No doubts defend?

Donald Davie

One flesh

Lying apart now, each in a separate bed,
He with a book, keeping the light on late,
She like a girl dreaming of childhood,
All men elsewhere – it is as if they wait
Some new event: the book he holds unread,
Her eyes fixed on the shadows overhead.

Tossed up like flotsam from a former passion,
How cool they lie. They hardly ever touch,
Or if they do, it is like a confession
Of having little feeling – or too much.
Chastity faces them, a destination
For which their whole lives were a preparation.

Strangely apart, yet strangely close together,
Silence between them like a thread to hold
And not wind in. And time itself's a feather
Touching them gently. Do they know they're old,
These two who are my father and my mother
Whose fire from which I came, has now grown cold?

Elizabeth Jennings

To her ancient lover

Ancient person, for whom I,
All the flattering youth defy;
Long be it e'er thou grow old,
Aching, shaking, crazy cold.
But still continue as thou art,
Ancient person of my heart.

On thy withered lips and dry,
Which like barren furrows lye;
Brooding kisses I will pour,
Shall thy youthful heat restore.
Such kind showers in autumn fall,
And a second spring recall:
Nor from thee will ever part,
Ancient person of my heart.

Thy nobler part, which but to name
In our sex would be counted shame,
By age's frozen grasp possessed,
From his ice shall be released,
And soothed by my reviving hand,
In former warmth and vigor stand.
All a lover's wish can reach,

For thy joy my love shall teach;
And for thy pleasure shall improve,
All that art can add to love.
Yet still I love thee without art,
Ancient person of my heart.

John Wilmot, Earl of Rochester

No one so much as you

No one so much as you
Loves this my clay,
Or would lament as you
Its dying day.
You know me through and through
Though I have not told,
And though with what you know
You are not bold.
None ever was so fair
As I thought you:
Not a word can I bear
Spoken against you.
All that I ever did
For you seemed coarse
Compared with what I hid
Nor put in force.
My eyes scarce dare meet you
Lest they should prove
I but respond to you
And do not love.
We look and understand,
We cannot speak
Except in trifles and
Words the most weak.
For I at most accept
Your love, regretting

That is all: I have kept
Only a fretting
That I could not return
All that you gave
And could not ever burn
With the love you have,
Till sometimes it did seem
Better it were
Never to see you more
Than linger here
With only gratitude
Instead of love -
A pine in solitude
Cradling a dove.

Edward Thomas

Index of first lines

Biographical notes

Compiled by the publishers

Kim Addonizio (1954–): Author of three books of poetry. Her latest collection, *What Is This Thing Called Love* was published in 2004. Addonizio currently teaches private poetry workshops in Oakland, California.

Anna Akhmatova (1889–1966): Russian lyric poet whose work achieved great popular success in Russia against all political odds. In 1964 and 1965 she was awarded the Etna-Taormina prize and an honorary doctorate from Oxford University.

Matthew Arnold (1822–1888): One of the legendary figures of Victorian poetry, he was Professor of Poetry at Oxford and was also Inspector of Schools for 35 years.

John Ashbery (1927–): Winner of the Pulitzer Prize, the National Book Critics Circle Award, and the National Book Award. His recent collection *Chinese Whispers* was published in 2003.

W. H. Auden (1907–1973): One of the most influential poets of the 20th century, he was born in England, but became an American citizen in 1946. His *Collected Poems* was published in 1991.

James K. Baxter (1926–1972): A central figure in New Zealand literature, he was a prolific writer, publishing more than 30 collections of poetry, plays, and literary criticism.

Thomas Lovell Beddoes (1803–1849): Educated at Oxford, he was a poet and dramatist whose poems were first published as a collected edition posthumously, in 1851.

John Berryman (1914–1972): Born in Oklahoma. A Pulitzer Prize winner, accomplished scholar, and respected teacher, his students included Philip Levine and Donald Justice. His *Collected Poems 1937–1971* was published in 1989.

Sujata Bhatt (1956–): Born in India. Bhatt has won a Commonwealth Poetry Prize, the Alice Hunt Bartlett Award, and received the Cholmondely Award in 1991.

Caroline Bird (1987–): *Looking Through Letterboxes,* the first collection by this young British poet was published in 2002, when she was only fifteen. She won the Poetry Society's Simon Elvin Young Poet of the Year Award two years running (2000/2001) and recently won an Eric Gregory award.

Elizabeth Bishop (1911–1979): Renowned American poet who won every major US poetry award, including the Pulitzer Prize and the National Book Award. *The Complete Poems 1927–1979* was published in 1983.

William Blake (1757–1827): Author of *Songs of Innocence* and *Songs of Experience.* Poet and engraver, now world famous for his visionary works, Blake's genius was not widely recognized in his day.

Louise Bogan (1897–1970): Born in Livermore Falls, Maine. She was poetry critic for *The New Yorker* for 38 years. Bogan published only 105 poems in her lifetime.

Eavan Boland (1944–): Born in Ireland. Boland is Professor of English at Stanford University. Recent collections include *Against Love Poetry* (2001), *The Lost Land* (1998), and *In a Time of Violence* (1994).

Anne Bradstreet (1612–1672): She emigrated to America in 1630, married Simon Bradstreet (a future governor of the Massachusetts colony), and had eight children. This did not stop her energetic writing activities—her first book of poems was published in London in 1650.

Robert Browning (1812–1889): Born in London. Renowned for his development of the dramatic monologue, Browning became one of the foremost Victorian poets. He eloped to Italy with the poet Elizabeth Barrett in 1846.

Elizabeth Barrett Browning (1806–1861): Famous for her widely anthologized *Sonnets from the Portuguese,* she was a prolific poet and translator. She married her fellow poet, Robert Browning.

Robert Burns (1759–1796): The national poet of Scotland, his poems and songs are written in Scottish dialect.

George Gordon, Lord Byron (1788–1824): Inventor of the romantic "Byronic hero." The publication of his first collection in 1812 made him an instant celebrity throughout Europe. He was forced to leave England in 1816 following a scandalous affair with his half-sister.

Lorna Dee Cervantes (1954–): Internationally acclaimed Mexican-American poet, her work focuses on the *chicana* woman's experience. She currently teaches at the University of Colorado.

Wendy Cope (1945–): Widely popular British poet. Her poetry collections include *Making Cocoa for Kingsley Amis* (1986), *Serious Concerns* (1992), and *If I Don't Know* (2001), which was shortlisted for the Whitbread Poetry Award. She lives in Winchester, England.

William Cowper (1731–1800): Despite bouts of depression and fragile mental health, he was well respected for his poetry and translations.

Hart Crane (1899–1932): Born in Garretsville, Ohio. His turbulent, unsettled life kept him constantly on the move. Crane was passionate about poetry, and the quest for his own poetic voice.

Stephen Crane (1871–1900): Known more as a novelist (particularly for *The Red Badge of Courage*) and journalist, he published one volume of poetry which received only posthumous praise. He died of tuberculosis at the age of 29.

e. e. cummings (1894–1962): Born in Cambridge, Massachusetts. He used experimental poetic forms and punctuation, and is admired for the playful spirit of his poetry.

J. V. Cunningham (1911–1985): Born in Cumberland, Maryland. He taught at Brandeis University until his retirement in 1980. *The Poems of J. V. Cunningham* was published in 1997.

Donald Davie (1922–1995): A highly regarded poet, translator, and critic, he published major studies of poetry. Davie taught at several American and British universities. His *Collected Poems* was published in 1990.

Emily Dickinson (1830–1886): A giant presence in 19th-century American poetry, with a highly original voice, she lived as a virtual recluse at her home in Amherst, Massachusetts. Only seven of her poems were published in her lifetime—her work was collected and published after her death.

John Donne (1572–1631): English author of sonnets, religious poems and essays as well as some marvelously erotic love poetry. He took holy orders in the Church of England in 1615.

H.D. (Hilda Doolittle) (1886–1961): Encouraged by the poet Ezra Pound, she moved to Europe in 1911 and became a prominent member of the expatriate American literary community.

Mark Doty (1953–): Acclaimed American poet, winner of many awards and fellowships in the US, also spanning the Atlantic to win the T. S. Eliot Prize in Britain. Doty has written extensively about the death of his lover from AIDS. He teaches at the University of Houston.

Keith Douglas (1920–1944): Killed during the invasion of Normandy, the poet had been previously injured after stepping on a land mine. He had prepared a collection of poetry for publication, but the book did not appear until 1966.

Ernest Christopher Dowson (1867–1900): He formed the Rhymers' Club in London, and was associated with the Decadent movement in France and England. Dowson was a longtime friend of Oscar Wilde.

Carol Ann Duffy (1955–): Acclaimed British poet, she is Professor of Poetry at Manchester Metropolitan University. Recent collections include *The World's Wife* (1999), *The Other Country* (1990), and *Mean Time* (1993).

Robert Duncan (1919–1988): Launched the *Experimental Review* with Sanders Russell, and became a leader of the San Francisco Renaissance and the group of poets associated with Black Mountain College. He taught at Black Mountain from 1956.

T. S. Eliot (1888–1965): Renowned for *The Waste Land* and *The Four Quartets,* he was also a foremost critic of the 20th century. Eliot was awarded the Nobel Prize in 1948. He founded the *Criterion* magazine.

Louise Glück (1943–): US Poet Laureate from 2003–2004, her collections include *The Seven Ages* (2001), *Meadowlands* (1996), *The Wild Iris* (1992), and *The Triumph of Achilles* (1985).

Robert Graves (1895–1985): British poet, novelist, essayist, he survived the Battle of the Somme in 1916, and eventually left England to live in Mallorca. His book *The White Goddess,* influenced generations of writers.

Thom Gunn (1929–2004): Born in England, he settled in San Francisco in 1960. Gunn taught at the University of California, Berkeley, as a Senior Lecturer in English. He published more than 30 books of poetry.

Marilyn Hacker (1942–): Born in New York City. She was editor of *The Kenyon Review* from 1990–1994, and has received numerous honors, including the National Book Award. She lives in New York City and Paris. Her most recent collection, *Desesperanto*, was published in 2003.

Donald Hall (1928–): Born in Connecticut. Hall was poetry editor of the *Paris Review.* Author of 15 books of poetry, and winner of many awards, he was married to fellow poet, the late Jane Kenyon. His recent collection *The Painted Bed* was published in 2002.

Sophie Hannah (1971–): British novelist and poet, she currently teaches at Manchester Metropolitan University's Writing School. Her most recent collection of poetry is *First of the Last Chances* (2003).

Thomas Hardy (1840–1928): He is probably better known for his novels, but dedicated the last 30 years of his life to poetry. Hardy wrote a series of exceptional love poems after the death of his first wife.

Gwen Harwood (1920–1995): A distinguished Australian poet, she won the Patrick White Award in 1978, and the Victoria Premier's Literary Award for Poetry in 1989. Her *Collected Poems* was published in 2003.

Robert Herrick (1591–1674): Born in London, he was honored as one of the finest English lyric poets. In 1623 Herrick took holy orders, and six years later became vicar of Dean Prior in Devonshire.

Alfred Edward Housman (1859–1936): Born in Worcestershire, he was educated at Oxford. His first (and probably best known) collection, *A Shropshire Lad*, was published in 1896.

Langston Hughes (1902–1967): Born in Joplin, Missouri. Poet, essayist, and writer of autobiography, fiction, and drama, Hughes was a prominent figure of the Harlem Renaissance. He published ten books of poetry, including *Montage of a Dream Deferred*.

Elizabeth Jennings (1926–2001): A renowned English poet, born in Lincolnshire, she studied at St. Anne's College, Oxford. Her *Collected Poems* was published in 1987.

Erica Jong (1942–): Famous for her bestselling novels, biography, and autobiography, she is also an accomplished poet. Jong received the United Nations Award for Excellence in Literature in 1998.

Ben Jonson (1572–1637): An associate of Shakespeare, Donne, and other eminent writers, he was a fine poet, playwright, translator, and critic. Jonson became the leading literary figure of his day.

Jane Kenyon (1947–1995): Appointed New Hampshire's Poet Laureate in 1995. She published four collections: *Constance* (1993), *Let Evening Come* (1990), *The Boat of Quiet Hours* (1986), and *From Room to Room* (1978).

Thomas Kinsella (1928–): Born in Ireland, he retired from the Civil Service in 1965 to teach in America. Kinsella now lives in Philadelphia. His *Collected Poems* was published in 2001.

Walter Savage Landor (1775–1864): Born at Ipsley Court, Warwick, he was educated at Trinity College, Oxford. Landor spent long periods in Italy, and died in Florence.

Emma Lazarus (1849–1887): She grew up in New York and Newport, Rhode Island, and was mentored by poet Ralph Waldo Emerson.

Denise Levertov (1923–1997): British-born but quintessentially American poet, she worked as a nurse in London during wartime. She emigrated to America in 1948 after she married writer Mitchell Goodman.

Federico García Lorca (1898–1936): A revered Spanish poet and dramatist, and member of the avant-garde Generation of 1927, he was killed by Nationalists at the start of the Spanish Civil War.

Robert Lowell (1917–1977): Received a Pulitzer Prize in 1946. The victim of serious psychological turmoil, he went on to publish *Life Studies* in 1959, which changed the landscape of modern American poetry.

Louis MacNeice (1907–1963): The Irish landscape of his childhood is a prominent aspect of his work. His *Autumn Journal,* published in 1938, chronicles the arrival of World War II in England.

Christopher Marlowe (1564–1593): As an Elizabethan dramatist he was second only to Shakespeare.

Andrew Marvell (1621–1678): Born in Yorkshire. Educated at Trinity College, Cambridge, he was known primarily as a satirist during his lifetime. Marvell's reputation as a great poet came only after his death— his poems were published posthumously.

Michael McClure (1932–): A scion of the Beat period, he joined Allen Ginsberg and friends at the famous Six Gallery reading in 1955, and for the "Human Be-In" of 1967.

W. S. Merwin (1927–): Born in New York City, he now lives and works in Hawaii. Merwin is a widely admired and respected poet and winner of the Pulitzer Prize amongst other awards. He is the author of many poetry books and plays, and has published nearly 20 books of translation, including Dante's *Purgatorio*.

Edna St. Vincent Millay (1892–1950): Born in Rockland, Maine, she moved to Greenwich Village and became part of its flourishing literary community. She won the Pulitzer Prize in 1923.

Pablo Neruda (1904–1973): Internationally acclaimed as the greatest Latin-American poet since Darío, he was awarded the International Peace Prize in 1950, the Lenin Peace Prize in 1953, and the Nobel Prize for Literature in 1971.

Henrik Nordbrandt (1945–): Danish poet who has lived for most of his life in the Mediterranean. In 2000, he received The Nordic Council Prize for Literature for *Drømmebroer* (*Dream Bridges*).

Naomi Shihab Nye (1952–): A Palestinian-American born in St. Louis, Missouri, she currently lives and works in San Antonio, Texas. Her poetry collections include *19 Varieties of Gazelle: Poems of the Middle East* (2002), *Fuel* (1998), *Red Suitcase* (1994), and *Hugging the Jukebox* (1982).

Sharon Olds (1942–): She was New York State Poet from 1998–2000. Recent titles include *The Unswept Room* (2003) and *Blood, Tin, Straw* (1999).

Wilfred Owen (1893–1918): He was born in Oswestry, Shropshire and enlisted in the army in 1915. While recuperating from shell shock he met Siegfried Sassoon and Robert Graves, who recognized his talent and encouraged his writing. Owen returned to the front and was killed in action in 1918. The posthumous collection, *Poems of Wilfred Owen*, was published in 1920 with an introduction by Siegfried Sassoon.

Dorothy Parker (1893–1967): Born in New Jersey. A legend of the 1920s and early 1930s, she wrote poems and features for *Vogue, Vanity Fair,* and *The New Yorker*. She later wrote screenplays and helped found the Screen Writers' Guild.

Boris Pasternak (1890–1960): Born in Moscow. A great Russian writer and poet, translator of many of Shakespeare's plays and author of *Doctor Zhivago*, he was awarded the Nobel Prize for Literature in 1958.

Kenneth Patchen (1911–1972): Born in Niles, Ohio. A prolific poet, painter and prose writer, Patchen wrote more than, 40 books of poetry, prose and drama. His *Collected Poems* was published in 1968.

Sylvia Plath (1932–1963): Born in Boston, Massachusetts and educated at Smith College and Newnham College, Cambridge. In England, Plath met and married the poet Ted Hughes. She published four collections, *The Colossus and Other Poems*, *Ariel*, *Crossing the Water*, and *Winter Trees*.

Ezra Pound (1885–1972): Influenced and promoted many writers, including T. S. Eliot and James Joyce. He coined the modernist motto, "make it new." Born in Idaho, he lived in Europe for most of his life. An edition of his famous *Cantos* was published in 1986.

Alexander Pushkin (1799–1837): Born in Moscow. One of the great Romantics, Pushkin is Russia's national poet, and is generally considered to be the founder of modern Russian literature. His best-known works include *Boris Godunov: A Drama in Verse*, *The Bronze Horseman*, and *Eugene Onegin*.

John Crowe Ransom (1888–1974): Born in Tennessee. Founder of the influential *Kenyon Review*, he helped to promote New Criticism, a critical approach that placed great emphasis on close textual scrutiny.

Kenneth Rexroth (1905–1982): A widely read writer, translator, and Buddhist-inspired poet, he laid the groundwork for the San Francisco Renaissance. Rexroth helped to found the San Francisco Poetry Center and organized meetings, readings, and poetry events.

Laura Riding Jackson (1901–1991): Born in New York City. Jackson was a prolific poet, novelist, and critic. She lived in Europe as well as in America. She published more than a dozen collections of poetry.

Arthur Rimbaud (1854–1891): Author of the renowned *Une Saison en Enfer* (*A Season in Hell*) and *Le Bateau Ivre* (*The Drunken Boat*), he was a poetic prodigy who was befriended and helped by fellow French poet Paul Verlaine. Verlaine published Rimbaud's complete works in 1895, securing the latter's fame.

Christina Rossetti (1830–1894): Sister of the poet and Pre-Raphaelite painter, Dante Gabriel Rossetti, she is best known for *Goblin Market, and Other Poems* (1862).

Muriel Rukeyser (1913–1980): Born in New York City. She was a dedicated poet and political activist, and her work focused on the inequalities of sex, race, and class. The volumes, *Out of Silence*, and *A Muriel Rukeyser Reader*, provide good introductions to her work.

Carl Sandburg (1878–): Born in Illinois. With the appearance of his *Chicago Poems* (1916), *Cornhuskers* (1918), *Smoke and Steel* (1920), and *Slabs of the Sunburnt West* (1922), his reputation was established. He received his second Pulitzer Prize for his *Complete Poems* in 1950. His final volumes of verse were *Harvest Poems, 1910–1960* (1960) and *Honey and Salt* (1963).

C. H. Sisson (1914–2003): Made Companion of Honor for services to literature in 1993, he was a prolific translator, poet, and essayist.

Wallace Stevens (1879–1955): Born in Pennsylvania. He worked in various law firms while writing poetry. Author of a dozen volumes of verse, his *Collected Poems* was published in 1990.

Mark Strand (1934–): Born on Prince Edward Island, Canada. Winner of many awards, he has served as Poet Laureate for the United States, and Chancellor of The Academy of American Poets. He is the author of ten books of poems, including *Blizzard of One* (1998), which won the Pulitzer Prize, *Dark Harbor* (1993), *The Continuous Life* (1990), *Selected Poems* (1980), *The Story of Our Lives* (1973), and *Reasons for Moving* (1968).

Sir John Suckling (1609–1642): "Cavalier" poet and playwright, he was described as the leading Gallant of his time, chiefly remembered for his grace and polished style.

Edward Thomas (1878–1917): Born in London. He greatly admired the poet Robert Frost who encouraged him to write after they met in 1913. All his poems were produced during the last few years of his life. Thomas died in action at the Battle of Arras, 1917.

Edmund Waller (1606–1687): Royalist exiled from England in 1643 for his part in a plot to secure London for the king, he was later an advocate of religious tolerance.

Richard Wilbur (1921–): He began writing poetry during the Second World War, when he served in Africa, France, and Italy. He won the Pulitzer Prize for Poetry with his *New and Collected Poems* (1988).

Oscar Wilde (1854-1900): Born in Ireland, he settled in London and became a renowned Victorian poet, playwright, and novelist.

William Carlos Williams (1883-1963): One of America's best-known poets. Winner of the National Book Award and the Pulitzer Prize, Williams was both a dedicated poet and a full-time physician. His poetry collections include *Journey to Love* and *The Broken Span*.

John Wilmot, Earl of Rochester (1647–1680): A favorite of Charles II and a leading court wit, he abducted the heiress Elizabeth Malet and was put in the Tower of London. He cut short his sentence by serving courageously in the second Dutch War.

Thomas Wyatt (1503–1542): Credited with introducing Italian sonnet forms to English literature in the 1530s, he was a diplomat in King Henry VIII's court.

Sources & Acknowledgements

Kim Addonizio: 'Stolen Moments' from *What Is This Thing Called Love: Poems* (W. W. Norton, 2004), by permission of the author; Anna Akhmatova: 'In Dream' translated by D. M. Thomas, from *Selected Poems of Anna Akhmatova* (Penguin Twentieth-Century Classics, 1992); John Ashbery: 'Some Trees' from *Selected Poems* (Carcanet Press, 1998); W. H. Auden: 'Lullaby' and 'Stop all the Clocks' from *Collected Shorter Poems 1927–1957* (Faber& Faber, 1969); James Baxter: 'Farewell to Jerusalem' from *Collected Poems of James K. Baxter,* edited by John Weir (Oxford University Press, 2004); John Berryman: 'Dream Song 4' from *Collected Poems, 1937–71* (Faber & Faber, 1991); Sujata Bhatt: 'Love in a Bathtub' from *Point No Point* (Carcanet Press, 2002), by permission of the publisher; Caroline Bird: 'Your Heartbreak' from *Looking Through Letterboxes* (Carcanet Press, 2002), by permission of the publisher; Elizabeth Bishop: 'The Shampoo' from *The Complete Poems 1927–1979* (The Hogarth Press, 1984), © 1979, 1983 by Alice Helen Methfessel; Louise Bogan: 'Words for Departure' from *The Blue Estuaries: Poems 1923–1968* (Viking Press, 1989); Eavan Boland: 'Love' from *Collected Poems* (Carcanet Press, 1995), by permission of the publisher; Anne Bradstreet: 'A Letter to Her Husband, Absent upon Publick Employment' from *Works* edited by Jeannine Hensley (Harvard University Press, 1981); Lorna Dee Cervantes: 'Y Volver' from *From the Cables of Genocide: Poems on Love and Hunger* (Arte Publico Press, 1991); Wendy Cope: 'Bloody Men' from *Serious Concerns* (Faber & Faber, 1992); E. E. Cummings: 'All in green went my love riding' from *Complete Poems 1904–1962,* edited by George J. Firmage (W. W. Norton, 1991), © 1991 by the Trustees for the E. E. Cummings Trust and George J. Firmage; J. V. Cunningham: 'To My Wife' from *The Poems of J. V. Cunningham* (Swallow Press, 1997); Emily Dickinson: 'We learned the Whole of Love' and 'Going to Him! Happy letter!' from *The Poems of Emily Dickinson,* edited by Thomas H. Johnson (Cambridge, Massachusetts: The Belknap Press of Harvard University Press), © 1951, 1955, 1979 by the President and Fellows of Harvard College; H. D. (Hilda Doolittle): 'Never more will the wind' from *Collected Poems: 1912–1944* (Carcanet Press, 1984), by permission of the publisher; Donald Davie: 'Time passing, beloved' from *Collected Poems* (Carcanet Press, 2002), by permission of the publisher; Mark Doty: 'The Embrace' from *Sweet Machine* (HarperFlamingo, 1999); Keith Douglas: 'The Prisoner' from *The Complete Poems* (Faber & Faber, 2001); Carol Ann Duffy: 'Girlfriends' from *The Other Country* (Anvil Press Poetry, 1990); Robert Duncan: 'Among my friends love is a great sorrow' from *Selected Poems* (Carcanet Press, 1993), by permission of the publisher; T. S. Eliot: 'La Figlia Che Piange' from *Collected Poems 1909–1962* (Faber & Faber, 1974); Louise Gluck: 'Happiness' from *First Five Books of Poems* (Carcanet

Press, 1997), by permission of the publisher; Robert Graves: 'Love Without Hope' and 'Counting the Beats' from *Complete Poems, in One Volume* (Carcanet Press, 2000), by permission of the publisher; Thom Gunn: 'The Hug' from *Collected Poems* (Faber & Faber, 1994); Marilyn Hacker: 'Villanelle' from *Selected Poems 1965–1990* (W. W. Norton, 1994); Donald Hall: 'Gold' from *Old and New Poems* (Ticknor & Fields, 1990), © 1990 by Donald Hall, by permission of Houghton Mifflin Company. All rights reserved; Sophie Hannah: 'Occupational Hazard' from *Leaving and Leaving You* (Carcanet Press, 1999), by permission of the publisher; Gwen Harwood: 'Carnal Knowledge II' from *Collected Poems* (Oxford University Press, 1991); A. E. Housman: 'Because I liked you better' from More Poems, XXXI, in *Collected Poems and Selected Prose* (Penguin Twentieth-Century Classics, 1989), by permission of The Society of Authors as the Literary Representative of the Estate of A. E. Housman; Langston Hughes: 'Juke Box Love Song' from *The Collected Poems of Langston Hughes* (Alfred A. Knopf, 1994), © 1994 by The Estate of Langston Hughes, by permission of David Higham Associates; Elizabeth Jennings: 'One Flesh' from *Collected Poems* (Macmillan, 1967), by permission of David Higham Associates; Erica Jong: 'Penis Envy' from *Becoming Light: Poems, New and Selected* (HarperPerennial, 1991); Jane Kenyon: 'Alone for a Week' from *Otherwise* (Graywolf Press, 1996); Thomas Kinsella: 'Soft, to Your Places' from *Collected Poems* (Carcanet Press, 2001), by permission of the publisher; Denise Levertov: 'The Ache of Marriage' from *Poems 1960–1967* (New Directions, 1983), © 1966 by Denise Levertov, by permission of the publisher; Federico Garcia Lorca: 'I Want' translated by Michael Schmidt, published by permission of Michael Schmidt; Robert Lowell: 'The Flaw' from *Collected Poems* (Faber & Faber, 2003); Michael McClure: 'Navajo Bracelet' from *Rebel Lions* (New Directions, 1991); Louis MacNeice: 'The Sunlight on the Garden' from *Collected Poems* (Faber & Faber, 1979), by permission of David Higham Associates; W. S. Merwin: 'Separation' from *The Moving Target* (Atheneum Publishers, 1963), © 1963 by W. S. Merwin; Edna St. Vincent Millay: 'Recuerdo' and 'Time does not bring relief; you all have lied' from *Collected Poems* (Harper & Row, 1956); Pablo Neruda: 'Poem 1' translated by W. S. Merwin, from *Twenty Love Poems and a Song of Despair* (Jonathan Cape, 1976); Henrik Nordbrandt: 'Sailing' translated by the author and Alexander Taylor, from *Egne digte* (Gyldendal, 2000); Naomi Shihab Nye: 'San Antonio' from *Is This Forever, or What?* (Harper/Greenwillow Books, 2004); Sharon Olds: 'Sex Without Love' from *The Dead and the Living* (Knopf, 1978), © 1987 by Sharon Olds, by permission of Alfred A. Knopf, a division of Random House Inc; Dorothy Parker: 'Love Song' and 'Two Cures for Love' from *The Collected Dorothy Parker* (Duckworth, 1973), by permission of the publisher; Boris Pasternak: 'The English Lesson' translated by Michael Schmidt, from *Selected Poems 1972–1997* by Michael Schmidt (Smith/Doorstop

Books, 1997), by permission of Michael Schmidt and the publisher; Kenneth Patchen: 'As We Are So Wonderfully Done With Each Other' from *Collected Love Poems of Kenneth Patchen* (Small Press Distribution, 1997); Sylvia Plath: 'The Couriers' from *Collected Poems* (Faber & Faber, 1981); Ezra Pound: 'Speech for Psyche in the Golden Book of Apuleius' from *Personae: The Shorter Poems of Ezra Pound,* edited by Lea Baechler and A. Walton Litz (New Directions, 1990); Alexander Pushkin: 'I loved you once' translated by Carol Ann Duffy, from *After Pushkin,* edited by Elaine Feinstein (Carcanet Press, 1999); John Crowe Ransom: 'Piazza Piece' from *Selected Poems* (Carcanet Press, 1991), by permission of the publisher; Kenneth Rexroth: 'Quietly' from *Complete Poems* (Copper Canyon Press, 2003); Laura Riding: 'A City Seems' from *The Poems of Laura Riding* (Carcanet Press, 1980), by permission of the publisher and the author's Board of Literary Management. In conformity with the late author's wish, her Board of Literary Management asks us to record that, in 1941, Laura (Riding) Jackson renounced, on grounds of linguistic principle, the writing of poetry: she had come to hold that 'poetry obstructs general attainment to something better in our linguistic way-of-life than we have'. Arthur Rimbaud: 'Romance' from *Rimbaud: Complete Works, Selected Letters* translated by W. Fowlie (University of Chicago Press, 2004), by permission of the publisher; Muriel Rukeyser: 'Waiting for Icarus' from *Collected Poems* (McGraw-Hill, 1978); Carl Sandburg: 'Bilbea' from *The Complete Poems of Carl Sandburg* (Harcourt Inc., 2003); C. H. Sisson: 'Pygmalion' from *Collected Poems* (Carcanet Press, 1998), by permission of the publisher; Wallace Stevens: 'Final Soliloquy of the Interior Paramour' from *Selected Poems* (Faber & Faber, 1965); Mark Strand: 'The Coming of Light' from *The Story of Our Lives* (Knopf, 2002), © 1971, 1972, 1973 by Mark Strand, by permission of Alfred A. Knopf, a division of Random House Inc; Richard Wilbur: 'Something Talking to Himself' from *Collected Poems 1943–2004* (Harcourt Inc., 2004); William Carlos Williams: 'Love Song' from *Collected Poems: 1909–1939, Volume 1,* © 1938 by New Directions Publishing Corporation, by permission of the publisher.

Every effort has been made to trace or contact copyright holders of the poems published in this book. The editor and publisher apologise for any material included without permission or without the appropriate acknowledgement, and would be glad to rectify any omissions brought to their attention at reprint.

Published by MQ Publications Limited

12 The Ivories, 6–8 Northampton Street

London N1 2HY

Tel: +44 (0) 20 7359 2244

Fax:+44 (0) 20 7359 1616

email: mail@mqpublications.com

website: www.mqpublications.com

ISBN: 1 84072 858 2

10 9 8 7 6 5 4 3 2 1

Printed and bound in China

Michael Schmidt

Michael Schmidt, poet, novelist and publisher, was born in Mexico City, and studied at Harvard and Oxford. He has created an internationally acclaimed poetry list at Carcanet Press, a leading UK literary publisher, where he is editorial and managing director. He is also Professor of English and Director of the Manchester Metropolitan University Writing School.

His published works include his collection *New and Selected Poems (1996), The Lives of the Poets* (1998), *The Harvill Book of Twentieth-Century Poetry In English* (2000), and *The Story of Poetry I, II, III, IV, V* (2001–2006). He edited *Elizabeth Jennings Collected Poems* (2003), and published *The First Poets: The Greeks* in 2004.